FALKLAND ISLANDS

TRAVEL GUIDE

2023 - 2024

A definitive guide to explore a beautiful mix of unspoilt scenery, rich history, and lively culture of the Nestled in the South Atlantic Ocean.

Kenneth Finley

Copyright

TABLE OF CONTENTS

1. INTRODUCTION

Welcome to the Falkland Islands

Nestled in the South Atlantic Ocean, the Falkland Islands are a secluded and picturesque location that invites adventurous tourists from across the globe. This archipelago, encompassing over 700 islands and islets, provides an unspoilt natural beauty and unique animal encounters that are nothing short of remarkable. Welcome to a country where penguins waddle along beautiful beaches, where mountainous terrain demands exploration, and where warm-hearted residents give a genuine welcome to those who journey to their shores.

About This Travel Guide

This thorough travel book is your key to uncovering the mysteries of the Falkland Islands, allowing you a look into the treasures that await you in this lonely colony. Whether you're an adventurous adventurer seeking animal encounters, a history buff captivated by the legends of this contested land, or just a visitor in quest of untouched natural beauty, this book is meant to cater to your every desire.

What Sets This Guide Apart?

We appreciate that your visit to the Falkland Islands is a voyage of a lifetime, and we've prepared this guide to assist you in making the most of every minute. Here's what distinguishes this tutorial apart:

1. Local Insights: This book is complemented with insights from residents who call the Falkland Islands home. Their knowledge and love for this wonderful area will enable you to view the two islands through their eyes.

2. Updated Information: It is devoted to presenting you with the most up-to-date information. While our knowledge cutoff date is September 2021, we have integrated projected changes and events for 2023-2024 to help you plan your trip successfully.

3. Detailed Itinerary: I have methodically created a 10-day travel itinerary that includes the finest of the Falkland Islands, ensuring you experience the essence of this place in a short period. From animal encounters to cultural events, our programme is your path to an amazing journey.

4. Insider advice: Discover hidden treasures and insider advice on where to locate the most fantastic animal encounters, coziest best local cafes, and the greatest hiking paths. Our objective is to make your Falkland Islands vacation unique.

5. Safety and Practical Advice: Your safety is our focus. We give vital safety information, including guidance on travel insurance, medical facilities, and emergency contacts. Plus, we give practical recommendations on what to carry, currency exchange, and visa needs.

6. Cultural Context: Gain a greater grasp of the Falkland Islands' history, culture, and legacy. Learn about the islanders' resiliency, their traditions, and the historical importance of the islands in the context of world geopolitics.

7. Sustainable Travel: As responsible travelers, we advocate sustainable behaviors. Find ideas on reducing your ecological imprint and protecting the sensitive environment of the Falkland Islands.

8. Future Updates: Our dedication doesn't stop here. We hope to publish an update for 2024, noting any new projects, events, or changes on the islands to ensure you have the freshest information at your fingertips.

Conclusion

As you begin your extraordinary voyage to the Falkland Islands, let this guide be your valued friend. Whether you're intrigued by the sounds of albatrosses, enthralled by the rugged beauty of the landscapes, or just seeking a calm respite from the hectic world, the Falkland Islands have something distinctive to offer. Prepare to be astonished, inspired, and fascinated by the hidden riches of this secluded island. Your Falkland Islands journey starts here.

2. PLANNING YOUR TRIP

When it comes to organizing a visit to the Falkland Islands, rigorous preparation is vital to ensuring a flawless and wonderful experience. In this part, we will look into the fundamental components of arranging your trip, including when to travel, visa and entrance procedures, currency concerns, and smart packing advice.

A. When to Visit

The Falkland Islands offer a peculiar climate characterized by erratic weather patterns, due to their position in the South Atlantic Ocean. The optimal time to visit primarily depends on your travel interests and the experiences you seek:

- **Summer (November to March):** This is the prime tourist season when the islands receive warmer weather and longer daylight hours. Wildlife aficionados will find this the optimum time for seeing penguins, seals, and seagulls. The negative is that lodgings may fill up fast, so it's wise to book well in advance.

- **Shoulder Seasons (April and October):** These months provide a balance between nice weather and fewer tourists. You may still enjoy animal interactions, although certain tourist amenities may have restricted hours or limited availability.

- **Winter (May to September):** While this season is marked by cooler temperatures and shorter days, it's a good period for birding, especially for aficionados looking to observe migrating species. It's also the most budget-friendly time to come, with reduced lodging costs.

B. Visa and Entry Requirements

Before going on your travel to the Falkland Islands, it's vital to understand the visa and admission requirements:

- **Tourist Visa**: Most visitors do not need a visa for trips of up to 90 days. However, it's vital to examine the precise criteria depending on your nationality, since visa laws might vary.

- **Passport**: Ensure your passport has at least six months of validity beyond your intended departure date from the Falkland Islands.

- **Immigration and Customs:** Be prepared for customs and immigration procedures upon arrival. Follow all restrictions and disclose any restricted or forbidden materials.

C. Currency and Budgeting

The official currency of the Falkland Islands is the Falkland Islands Pound (FKP), which is pegged to the British Pound (GBP) at a 1:1 exchange rate. While credit cards are frequently accepted in Stanley (the capital), it's smart to bring some cash for purchases in more rural places. ATMs are available in Stanley but may not be accessible on smaller islands.

Budgeting for your Falkland Islands vacation might vary greatly based on your travel style. Accommodation, food, and activities might be pricey, therefore it's essential to prepare accordingly:

- **Accommodation**: Hotels and lodges are the principal alternatives in Stanley, with costs ranging depending on location and comfort level. Camping is a budget-friendly choice for the adventurous.

- **Meals:** Dining in the Falkland Islands may be pricey owing to the remote location of the islands. Local restaurants provide wonderful seafood but be prepared for higher pricing.

- **Activities**: Excursions and trips to watch animals and discover the islands' beauty may come with extra expenses. It's important to reserve them in advance to ensure your position.

D. Packing Tips

Packing for the Falkland Islands needs considerable planning owing to the unpredictable weather conditions:

- **Clothing**: Layering is crucial. Pack warm gear, especially waterproof coats and sturdy footwear for outdoor activities. Even in July, temperatures may be frigid.

- **Gear**: Binoculars and a decent camera are necessary for wildlife lovers. Don't forget a power adapter if you have electrical gadgets.

- **Prescriptions**: Bring any required prescriptions, since access to pharmacies may be restricted outside of Stanley.

- **Travel Insurance:** Invest in comprehensive travel insurance that covers medical emergencies and trip cancellations. It's a safety net for unanticipated occurrences.

By considering five key areas of arranging your Falkland Islands tour, you'll be well-prepared to make the most of your visit to this distant and interesting region. Whether you're exploring the outdoors, marveling at animals, or immersing yourself in the culture, your vacation to the Falkland Islands promises to be a once-in-a-lifetime experience.

3. GETTING THERE

Traveling to the Falklands is an adventure in itself, considering its isolated position in the South Atlantic Ocean. While the islands are not readily accessible, there are solid choices for visiting this wonderful site.

A. Flights to the Falkland Islands

Stanley, the capital of the Falkland Islands, is serviced by the Mount Pleasant Airport (MPA), the principal entrance to the archipelago. Here's all you need to know about flights to the Falklands:

- **International links**: To visit the Falkland Islands, passengers often take international flights to one of the adjacent countries having direct links to MPA. The most popular departure places were Santiago (Chile), Punta Arenas (Chile), and São Paulo (Brazil).

- **Airline Options:** The Falkland Islands Government Air Service (FIGAS) conducts flights to and from MPA. The travel routes and timetables often change, so it's crucial to plan your trip carefully and check flight availability well in advance.

- **Travel Time**: The flight length might vary based on your departure city. For example, the trip from Santiago, Chile, to Mount Pleasant Airport takes roughly 4 to 5 hours.

- **Baggage limitations**: Pay attention to baggage limitations, since certain flights to the Falkland Islands have weight limits for both checked and carry-on bags.

- **Weather Considerations**: Due to the Falklands' unpredictable weather, flight plans might be subject to modification. It's recommended to allow some flexibility in your trip arrangements.

B. Travelling Sea

For those wanting a new and exciting method to visit the Falkland Islands traveling fats provide an alternate choice. Here's what you should know about this seafaring journey:

- **Cruise Ships**: Some cruise lines include the Falkland Islands in their itineraries. Travelers may embark on a cruise from several South American ports, such as

Ushuaia in Argentina or Punta Arenas in Chile. These trips frequently allow the option to visit other isolated sites in the area, including Antarctica.

- **Ferry Services**: The Falkland Islands Government offers a ferry service known as the MV Concordia Bay, which links East Falkland to West Falkland. This boat is mainly utilized for moving products and people between the islands, giving a unique chance to experience local life and enjoy stunning sights along the trip.

- **Yacht & Sailboat Travel**: For the most daring and independent visitors, traveling to the Falkland Islands on private yachts or sailboats is an alternative. However, this needs careful preparation, experience in sailing, and obedience to maritime rules.

- **Customs and Immigration**: Regardless of the manner of maritime passage, tourists must follow customs and immigration procedures upon arriving in the Falkland Islands. Ensure you have all appropriate papers, including passports and visas.

Conclusion

Whether you choose to arrive in the Falkland Islands by air or boat, travel to this isolated and wonderful region is a vital part of the experience. While flights to Mount Pleasant Airport provide convenience and are the most frequent alternative for guests, touring the islands by ship gives a distinct perspective on the region's raw beauty and nautical culture. Whichever path you choose, your arrival in the Falkland Islands promises to be the beginning of an unforgettable trip in this pure and undisturbed corner of the globe.

4. ACCOMMODATION

Accommodations in the Falkland Islands cater to a variety of inclinations, from those seeking the conveniences of hotels and resorts to adventurous tourists who prefer camping under the starry sky. Additionally, guesthouses and beautiful bed & and breakfasts provide an insight into the wonderful hospitality of the Falkland Islanders. Here's a deeper look at your options:

A. Hotels and Lodges

Hotels and lodges are the major options for tourists who value the ease and comfort of contemporary facilities. In Stanley, the capital of the Falkland Islands, you'll find various lodging alternatives to pick from:

- **Malvina House Hotel**: Offering stunning views of Stanley Harbor, this hotel has comfortable accommodations, a restaurant offering local cuisine, and a pleasant bar for restful nights.

- **The Waterfront Boutique Hotel and café**: With a fantastic position along the waterfront, this boutique hotel has lovely accommodations, a delightful café, and helpful personnel to assist with your requirements.

- **Sparrow Cove House:** A lodge-style lodging on East Falkland, it gives a calm getaway with breathtaking surroundings, kind hospitality, and snug accommodations.

B. Camping Options

For the adventurous tourist seeking to immerse oneself in the Falklands' untamed splendor, camping is a popular and cost-effective solution. Here are some camping alternatives to consider:

- **Bertha's Beach campsite**: Located on East Falkland, this campsite provides limited amenities and access to the pristine Bertha's Beach, famed for its animals and spectacular panoramas.

- **Cape Bougainville Camping Pods**: These snug pods give a protected camping experience with vital conveniences like heating and cooking facilities. They're positioned on East Falkland, making it easy for exploration.

- **Volunteer Point camping:** If you're focused on watching colonies of king penguins, this camping near Volunteer

Point on East Falkland is a wonderful option. Be prepared for limited amenities and magnificent animal encounters.

C. Guesthouses and B&Bs

Staying in guesthouses or bed and breakfasts (B&Bs) in the Falkland Islands allows engaging with local locals and enjoying the island's warm and hospitable culture:

- **Fitzroy Farm Cottage**: Located on East Falkland, this quaint cottage provides a peaceful refuge with self-catering services. The hosts give important insights into life in the Falklands.

- **Gypsy Cove House**: Nestled in a calm area, this guesthouse offers comfortable accommodations and spectacular views. It's a wonderful site for birdwatchers and environment aficionados.

- **Sea LiResortort:** Situated on Sea Lion Island, this resort provides comfortable accommodations with spectacular ocean views. It's a heaven for nature enthusiasts, with many opportunities to see seals, sea lions, and birds.

D. Booking in Advance

It's crucial to know that lodgings in the Falkland Islands, particularly during the high summer season, may fill up rapidly. your stay, especially in hotels and lodges, it's essential to make bookings well in advance.

Whether you select a hotel for contemporary conveniences, camping for a raw adventure, or a guesthouse/B&B for a more personal encounter, lodgings in the Falkland Islands are intended to improve your entire travel experience. Each choice gives a unique approach to engaging with the islands' natural beauty and the warm-hearted residents who call the Falklands home.

5. EXPLORING STANLEY: The Heart of the Falkland Islands

As the capital of the Falkland Islands, Stanley is not simply the political and economic center but also a hub for cultural experiences, and history, and a gateway to the natural beauties that the island provides. In this detailed guide, we will take you on a tour around Stanley, offering insights into discovering this delightful town, seeing its historical attractions, and experiencing its eating and nightlife scene.

A. Discovering the Capital

Stanley is the biggest and most populated settlement in the Falkland Islands, with a population of roughly 2,500 inhabitants. Despite its distant position in the South Atlantic Ocean, Stanley boasts a particular appeal that captivates travelers from across the globe.

- **Stanley Harbor**: Begin your journey with a walk around the gorgeous Stanley Harbor, where colorful buildings line the shore. It's a terrific area to take shots and absorb in a casual environment.

- **Anglican Cathedral** : This renowned church is not only the southernmost Anglican cathedral in the world but also sports an uncommon feature—a whalebone arch constructed from the jaws of two blue whales. It's an important emblem of the Falkland Islands.

- **Falkland Islands Museum and National Trust**: Delve into the history and culture of the Falklands at this museum. It has amazing displays on everything from early settlers to the 1982 war.

- **Government House:** Although not available to the public, you may appreciate the architecture of the official house of the Governor of the Falkland Islands, which overlooks Stanley Harbor.

B. Historical Sites

Stanley's rich history is entwined with the Falkland Islands' past, especially its participation in the 1982 battle. Exploring historical places is a requirement for everyone interested in the islands' past.

- **Battle Memorial**: Commemorating the lives lost during the Falklands War in 1982, the Battle Memorial serves as a heartbreaking reminder of the conflict's effect on the islands and its inhabitants.

- **Falkland Islands Defence Force Museum:** This museum gives insights into the history of the Falkland Islands Defence Force, which played a vital part in the islands' defense throughout the war.

- **Government House grounds**: While you can't visit Government House, you may tour it's lovely grounds, which are accessible to the public. They provide a calm location with breathtaking views.

C. Dining and Nightlife

Stanley may be a tiny town, but it provides a surprising range of food choices and a pleasant nightlife scene that enables you to relax after a day of exploring.

- **The Waterfront café:** Located near the waterfront, this café is noted for its fresh seafood dishes, including locally caught fish and squid. Enjoy a dinner while marveling at the waterfront views.

- **Upland Goose Hotel & Restaurant**: The Upland Goose is a pleasant venue for eating, featuring a blend of foreign and Falklands-inspired food. Don't miss sampling the Falklands lamb, famed for its quality and flavor.

- **Victory Bar**: For a taste of the local bar culture, Victory Bar is a popular option. It's a terrific spot to mix with locals and other visitors, with a range of beers and spirits.

- **Malvina House Hotel Bar**: The Malvina House Hotel's bar is a welcome area to have a drink, typically offering live music and a friendly environment.

- **The Trough Restaurant**: A casual eating choice with a calm ambience, The Trough delivers comfort cuisine including burgers, sandwiches, and substantial breakfasts.

- **Nightlife**: While Stanley may not have a booming nightlife scene, you can find several welcoming pubs and bars where you can have a nightcap and speak with locals and other tourists. Keep in mind that many places have restricted late-night hours.

In conclusion, touring Stanley is a vital element of any visit to the Falkland Islands. This lovely city, with its ancient landmarks, scenic harbor, and hospitable population, provides a doorway to discovering the distinctive culture and history of the Falklands. Whether you're meandering along the shoreline, immersing yourself in history, eating local food, or enjoying the snug nightlife, Stanley provides something for any tourist seeking a genuine experience in this distant and lovely place.

6. WILDLIFE AND NATURE

The Falkland Islands are a delight for environment enthusiasts and animal aficionados. This secluded archipelago, situated in the South Atlantic Ocean, features a diversity of unusual animals and vegetation, making it a great location for birding and whale watching. Let's discover the enchanting world of animals and environment in the Falkland Islands.

A. Unique Fauna and Flora

One of the Falkland Islands' distinguishing qualities is its incredible biodiversity, which includes species found nowhere else on Earth. Here are some highlights of the islands' biodiversity and flora:

- **Penguins**: The Falklands are home to many kinds of penguins, including

Gentoo, Rockhopper, King, and Magellanic penguins. These beautiful birds may be found breeding throughout the beaches, affording wonderful possibilities for up-close encounters.

- **Albatrosses**: The islands provide a crucial breeding site for various albatross species, with the Wandering Albatross being the most iconic. Witnessing these huge seabirds flying on the breezes is a stunning sight.

- **Seals and Sea Lions**: Falklands' seas are frequented by seals and sea lions, notably the Southern Elephant Seal and South American Sea Lion. Watch them sunbathe in the sun on secluded beaches or dive elegantly in search of food.

- **Diverse Birdlife**: Birdwatchers will be in awe of the Falkland Islands' great bird variety. From the colorful and humorous Striated Caracara to the magnificent Falkland Steamer Duck, the islands provide a wealth of bird species to view.

- **Unique Flora**: While the islands' flora may not be as well-known as its animals, you'll discover diverse plant life suited to the severe environment. Look out for local flora like the Falkland Islands' Pale Maiden and native grasses that cover the terrain.

B. Birdwatching

Birdwatchers from across the globe consider the Falkland Islands a must-visit location owing to its exceptional bird population. Here's all you need to know about birding in this distant paradise:

- **Best Viewing Locations**: Several places across the Falkland Islands give great birding possibilities. Volunteer Point on East Falkland is famed for its king penguin colonies, whereas West Point Island is recognised for its albatross rookeries.

- **Guided excursions:** Consider attending guided birding excursions to get the most out of your experience. Knowledgeable guides can assist in identifying species and give intriguing information about Falklands' birds.

- **Photography**: Bird photography is a popular activity in the Falklands, so don't forget your camera and a decent zoom lens to capture the great variety of birds.

C. Whale Watching

Whale watching in the Falklands allows observation of the ocean's most stunning animals in their natural environment. Key aspects concerning whale watching include:

- **Season**: The greatest period for whale viewing is during the Australian summer, from November to March when many whale species come to the Falklands' seas to feed and spawn.

- **Species**: Common whale species you may meet include Orcas (killer whales), Southern Right Whales, and Minke Whales, among others. Dolphins, such as

Commerson's Dolphins, are also regularly spotted.

- **Tour companies:** Several tour companies in the Falklands provide whale-watching tours. These trips give a sensible and polite method to watch these aquatic giants without upsetting them.

In conclusion, the Falkland Islands are a refuge for animals and environmental aficionados. The archipelago's distinctive wildlife and flora, together with its superb birding and whale-watching possibilities, make it a destination like no other. Whether you're charmed by the sight of penguins waddling on beautiful beaches or the excitement of watching whales breaking the ocean's surface, the

Falkland Islands provide a fully immersive and unique natural experience.

7. OUTDOOR ADVENTURES

The Falkland Islands, with their rough and beautiful landscapes, offer a multitude of outdoor opportunities for anyone wishing to explore the great outdoors. From hiking and trekking over stunning terrains to fishing and angling in the copious seas, and scuba diving in the rich marine ecology, there's no lack of fascinating activities to be experienced.

A. Hiking & Trekking

Hiking and hiking aficionados will discover the Falkland Islands to be a hidden treasure. The archipelago's different landscapes provide a multitude of routes and pathways to explore:

- **Mount Usborne**: As the highest summit in the Falklands, Mount Usborne presents a demanding journey with magnificent panoramic views of East Falklands scenery.

- **Volunteer Point**: Known for its spectacular coastal beauty and plentiful animals, Volunteer Point provides a reasonably simple climb. Along the route, you'll meet colonies of king penguins, Magellanic penguins, and other seabirds.

- **Cape Bougainville**: On East Falkland, Cape Bougainville provides lovely seaside treks. The Cape's lighthouse and the surrounding surroundings give good possibilities for birding.

- **Bertha's Beach**: This is an accessible and family-friendly hiking location with a route leading to a lovely sandy beach where you may watch elephant seals and other marine life.

B. Fishing and Angling

The Falkland Islands are a dream location for fishing and angling aficionados, with extensive chances for both beach and boat fishing:

- **Deep-Sea Fishing**: The seas around the Falklands are rich with marine life. Deep-sea fishing tours give the possibility to capture species including sea bass, halibut, and many varieties of cod.

- **Fly Fishing**: For those interested in fly fishing, the Falkland Islands are home to magnificent rivers and streams where you may cast your line for brown trout and sea-run trout.

- **Rockhopper Fishing**: One of the unique fishing experiences in the Falklands is rockhopper fishing, where you may target rockhopper species like the Magellanic Rockhopper and the Yellow-nosed Albatross.

C. Scuba Diving

Scuba diving in the Falkland Islands gives a chance to discover the diverse marine ecology under the surface:

- **Marine Life:** Dive into crystal-clear waters to experience a diversity of marine life, including seals, sea lions, dolphins, and many types of fish. The Falklands are also noted for their kelp forests and colorful underwater beauty.

- **Wreck Diving:** Explore shipwrecks going back to the 19th and 20th centuries, offering a fascinating peek into the islands' nautical past.

- **Diving destinations:** Some popular diving destinations are New Island, Kidney Island, and the seas near Stanley. Be prepared for varied water temperatures and strong currents, making advanced diving certification desirable.

Whether you're trekking to gorgeous vistas, throwing your line into rich fishing grounds, or sinking into the depths for a scuba diving excursion, the Falkland Islands offer a broad choice of outdoor activities that appeal to explorers of all abilities. With its undisturbed natural beauty and rare animal encounters, the

Falklands guarantee an amazing outdoor experience in a remote and pristine area.

8. CULTURAL EXPERIENCES

While the Falkland Islands are recognised for their spectacular natural landscapes and exceptional wildlife, they also offer an assortment of engaging cultural activities that give insight into the distinctive way of life and rich history of the inhabitants. From visiting local towns and digging into Falkland Islands history to exploring the flourishing arts and crafts sector, cultural aficionados will find lots to learn.

A. Visiting Local Communities

Engaging with the warm-hearted inhabitants is one of the most gratifying cultural experiences in the Falkland Islands. The Islanders, nicknamed "Kelpers," are recognised for their warm hospitality and fondness for sharing their tales and traditions:

- **Tea with a Local**: The Falkland Islanders' custom of afternoon tea is a fantastic opportunity to connect with the community. Joining a local family for tea is an opportunity to hear firsthand tales of life on the islands, their history, and personal experiences.

- **Community activities**: Keep an eye out for community activities and gatherings, such as local fairs, sports matches, and music performances. Participating in these activities gives a real peek into Falthe klands' culture.

- **Small villages**: Venture beyond Stanley to explore small villages and distant communities on the several islands. These trips enable you to experience the modest but robust way of life of the islanders.

B. Falkland Islands History

Understanding the history of the Falkland Islands is crucial to comprehending the culture and identity of its people. Exploring historical buildings and museums gives an interesting peek into the archipelago's past:

- **Falkland Islands Museum and National Trust:** Located in Stanley, this museum has a plethora of items and displays that dive into the islands' history, from early colonization through the Falklands War in 1982.

- **Battlefields and monuments:** Visiting historical battlefields and monuments gives a chance to pay respects to the lives lost during the Falklands War. These places give profound insights into the islands' more recent past.

- **Historic Buildings:** Stroll around Stanley and admire the lovely historic buildings, some of which date back to the 19th century. The colonial architecture is a testimony to the islands' past.

C. Arts and Crafts

The Falkland Islands feature a flourishing arts and crafts culture, exhibiting the ingenuity and ability of its population. These cultural forms are profoundly entrenched in the Falkland Islands' natural surroundings:

- **Art Galleries**: Visit local art galleries in Stanley to examine works by Falkland

Islands artists. Many of these paintings take inspiration from the spectacular scenery and animals of the islands.

- **Craft Markets**: Craft markets allow acquiring handcrafted souvenirs and presents, including jewelry and ceramics, produced by local craftsmen. These objects frequently represent the Falklands' particular character.

- **Creative Workshops**: Some artists and crafters in the Falklands provide workshops and courses. Participating in these programmes enables you to learn about traditional crafts and make your own unique items.

In conclusion, the Falkland Islands' cultural experiences create a stronger connection to the people, history, and creative manifestations of this distant island. Engaging with local people, experiencing historical landmarks, and immersing yourself in arts and crafts give a well-rounded picture of the Falklands' culture and legacy. These activities, along with the islands' natural charms, make a really rewarding vacation for guests seeking a comprehensive grasp of this unique place.

9. TRAVEL ITINERARY

A. 10-Day Adventure in the Falkland Islands

Embarking on a 10-day tour in the Falkland Islands offers an exciting voyage packed with animal encounters, outdoor activities, cultural discovery, and stunning vistas. Here's a full schedule to help you get the most out of your Falklands experience:

Day 1-2: Arrival in Stanley

Day 1: Arrival in Stanley

- Arrive at Mount Pleasant Airport (MPA), where you'll be welcomed with the breathtaking scenery of East Falkland.
- Transfer to Stanley, the capital, and check into your selected lodgings.

- Explore the lovely Stanley Harbor, with its colorful residences and old buildings.
- Enjoy a leisurely evening at one of the local eateries, tasting fresh seafood.

Day 2: Stanley Exploration

- Begin your day with a visit to Christ Church Cathedral, home of the famed whalebone arch.
- Immerse yourself in Falkland Islands history with a tour to the Falkland Islands Museum and National Trust.
- Take a walk through Government House Gardens, appreciating the well-maintained vegetation.
- Sample local food at one of Stanley's quaint places, such as the Waterfront Bistro.

Day 3-4: Wildlife Encounters

Day 3: King Penguin Encounter

- Start your wildlife excursion with a day's journey to Volunteer Point on East Falkland.
- Witness large colonies of king penguins, Magellanic penguins, and other seabirds.
- Enjoy a picnic lunch among the gorgeous coastline views.
- Return to Stanley in the evening for a well-deserved relaxation.

Day 4: Albatross Rookeries

- Embark on an expedition to West Point Island, noted for its albatross rookeries.
- Observe these gorgeous seabirds in their natural environment.

- Explore the island's stunning scenery and explore the West Point Island Lodge.
- Return to Stanley, where you may lunch at the Upland Goose Hotel and Restaurant.

Day 5-6: Outdoor Adventures

Day 5: Hiking and Exploration

- Gear up for an outdoor adventure by trekking to the top of Mount Usborne, the highest mountain in the Falkland Islands.
- Revel in panoramic vistas of East Falkland's sceneries.
- Spend the night camping in the outdoors to connect with nature.

Day 6: Coastal Treks

- After breaking camp, proceed on coastal excursions along the rough beach.
- Keep a watch out for seals, sea lions, and numerous bird species.
- Return to Stanley, where you may relax with a supper at a local restaurant.

Day 7-8: Cultural Exploration

Day 7: Local Communities

- Take a day excursion to a tiny village or isolated community to connect with the friendly islanders.
- Share tea with a local family to learn about their way of life and hear intriguing tales.

- Participate in any community activities or gatherings going place during your stay.

Day 8: Falkland Islands History

- Dive into Falkland Islands history with a tour of key battlefields and monuments.
- Explore the colonial architecture of Stanley's historic buildings.
- Reflect on the Falklands War at the Battle Memorial.
- Enjoy supper at the Victory Bar, a neighborhood tavern where you may interact with neighbors.

Day 9-10: Farewell to the Falklands
Day 9: Arts & Crafts

- Explore Stanley's art galleries and artisan markets to appreciate local talent.

- Attend creative classes if offered, where you may try your hand at traditional crafts.
- Shop for items including handcrafted jewelry, knitwear, and ceramics.

Day 10: Departure

- Say goodbye to the Falkland Islands with a heart full of memories.
- Depart from Mount Pleasant Airport (MPA) with a better respect for the islands' natural beauty, distinct culture, and warm-hearted population.

This 10-day vacation in the Falkland Islands offers a broad and engaging experience, combining animal encounters, outdoor exploration, cultural involvement, and historical insights. It's an itinerary intended to make the most of your stay in this lonely and enchanting region, leaving you with treasured memories and a meaningful connection to the Falklands.

10. 2024 UPDATES

As you plan your vacation to the Falkland Islands in 2024, you'll discover that this distant island continues to provide its distinctive combination of unspoiled scenery, plentiful wildlife, and kind hospitality. In this update, we'll highlight what's new in the Falkland Islands for the year 2024, give information on interesting events and festivals, and provide crucial travel suggestions for the new year.

A. What's New in the Falkland Islands

The Falkland Islands have been actively attempting to improve the tourist experience while protecting their natural beauty. Here are some important changes for 2024:

- **Sustainable tourism Initiatives:** The Falkland Islands are dedicated to sustainable tourism practices. New measures include tougher limits for animal watching and attempts to reduce the environmental effect of tourist operations.

- **Improved lodgings**: While keeping the islands' secluded and wild nature, numerous lodgings in Stanley and beyond have undergone repairs and modifications, bringing additional comfort and convenience to guests.

- **Enhanced connection:** The Falklands have continued to strengthen their connection. Visitors should anticipate more dependable internet access and greater mobile phone service in certain regions.

- **Local Cuisine:** Falklands' cuisine is changing, with an increased concentration on locally derived foods. Look out for restaurants and diners providing meals created with fresh Falklands lamb, shellfish, and other island ingredients.

B. Events and Festivals in 2024

The Falkland Islands are noted for their strong community spirit and cultural festivities. Here are some events and festivals you can look forward to in 2024:

- **Falkland Islands Marathon (March):** Lace up your running shoes for the Falkland Islands Marathon, where competitors may enjoy the picturesque splendor of Stanley and its surroundings while competing in several race categories.

- **Falkland Islands Music Festival (April):** This yearly festival celebrates local musical talent, with performances ranging from classical to contemporary. It's a terrific chance to immerse oneself in the local artistic scene.

- **Falkland Islands Agricultural Show (November):** Experience a genuine flavor of Falklands life at the Agricultural Show, with livestock shows, crafts, local food, and lots of entertainment for the entire family.

- **Christmas Festivities (December):** Celebrate the holiday season Falklands-style, with Christmas markets, carol singing, and seasonal decorations across Stanley.

C. Travel Tips for the New Year

As you plan your journey to the Falkland Islands in 2024, consider the following travel recommendations to make the most of your experience:

- **Booking in Advance**: Due to the limited availability of hotels and guided tours, it's advised to plan your stay and excursions well in advance, particularly during the busy summer season.

- **Pack for All Seasons**: The Falklands' weather may be unpredictable. Pack layers, waterproof clothes, and sturdy walking boots for outdoor activities.

- **Respect Wildlife:** When witnessing wildlife, stick to standards and keep a respectful distance to reduce disruption to the animals.

- **Stay Informed**: Keep up to speed with any travel limitations, visa requirements, and health and safety rules, which might change.

- **Travel Insurance:** Invest in comprehensive travel insurance that covers medical emergencies and unexpected trip delays.

The Falkland Islands continue to be a destination of extraordinary natural beauty and cultural depth. As you discover what's new, attend festivals and events, and follow this travel advice, your visit to the Falklands in 2024 promises to be an exciting and unforgettable experience.

11. TRAVEL RESOURCES

When going to the Falkland Islands, it's crucial to have access to reputable travel resources to guarantee a smooth and pleasurable experience. Here, we give information on crucial contacts, handy applications and websites, and safety advice to assist you throughout your stay.

A. Important Contacts

Falkland Islands Government Tourist Board: The official tourist authority can give helpful information regarding travel, lodgings, and activities in the Falkland Islands. Contact them for information and advice on organizing your trip.

- **Website**: Falkland Islands Tourist Board Email: info@falklandislands.com

- **Emergency Services:** In case of emergency, including medical or police help, telephone 999 (inside the Falkland Islands) or 112 (from mobile phones).

- **Mount Pleasant Airport (MPA):** For flight information, lost luggage, or airport questions, contact MPA.

- **Website**: Mount Pleasant Airport Email: mpa_airport@sec.gov.fk
- **Phone**: +500 72229
- **Consular Services**: If you are a foreign citizen, contact your country's embassy or consulate in the United Kingdom for help with travel-related matters while in the Falkland Islands.

B. Useful Apps and Websites

Falklands Conservation App: This app includes information about animals, trails, and conservation projects in the Falkland Islands. It's a wonderful resource for wildlife aficionados.

- **Available on**: Android and iOS
- **Stanley Walking Tour App**: Explore Stanley, the capital of the Falkland Islands, with this self-guided walking tour app. It gives historical information and emphasizes local sites.

- **Available on:** Android and iOS Weather applications: Stay current on Falklands' weather conditions with popular weather applications like AccuWeather, The Weather Channel, or local meteorological websites.

- **Google Maps**: While internet availability may be restricted in certain regions, offline maps on Google Maps may help you traverse the islands, particularly in Stanley.

- **TripAdvisor**: Check reviews and suggestions for lodgings, restaurants, and activities from other visitors on TripAdvisor.

- **Falkland Islands Government Website:** The government's official website offers crucial information for tourists, including visa requirements, customs restrictions, and local news.

- **Website**: Falkland Islands Government Safety Information

- **Health and Medical Care**: The Falkland Islands have a hospital in Stanley with medical services. It's crucial to have comprehensive travel insurance that covers medical situations.

- **Wildlife Safety**: When witnessing wildlife, keep a respectful distance to prevent upsetting animals. Follow recommendations set by trip providers and guides.

- **Weather Conditions**: Be prepared for shifting weather conditions, particularly if you plan outside activities. Dress in layers, pack waterproof clothes and carry basics like water, food, and a first-aid kit.

- **Emergency Services:** Save emergency contact numbers, such as 999 for medical and police issues, on your phone. Ensure your hotel has clear emergency exit information.

- **Internet and Communication:** Internet connectivity might be restricted in certain locations of the Falkland Islands. Inform someone of your vacation intentions and projected return times if you want to visit isolated regions.

- **Currency and Payments:** The currency used in the Falkland Islands is the Falkland Islands Pound (FKP). Ensure you have adequate local currency for costs, since credit card acceptance may be restricted.

- **Responsible tourist:** Adhere to responsible tourism principles, such as avoiding disturbing animals or littering. Respect the environment and the local culture.

By using these travel resources, including vital contacts, handy apps and websites, and safety information, you can make the most of your visit to the Falkland Islands while keeping informed, safe, and well-prepared for the unique experiences this isolated region has to offer.

CONCLUSION

As you begin on the trek to the Falkland Islands, you are stepping into a world unlike any other. This secluded island, located in the South Atlantic Ocean, provides a tapestry of experiences that span a pristine environment, amazing animal encounters, rich cultural inquiry, and warm-hearted hospitality. Your Falkland Islands vacation promises to be an extraordinary and transforming excursion.

From the minute you arrive in Stanley, the picturesque capital, through the days spent trekking in mountainous terrain, viewing penguins, albatrosses, and seals, and connecting with the hospitable local inhabitants, you'll find yourself immersed in the Falklands' particular appeal.

Whether you're an outdoor enthusiast, a nature lover, a history buff, or an admirer of art and culture, the Falkland Islands have something to offer every tourist. The 2024 changes reflect the archipelago's commitment to sustainability and increasing the tourist experience, ensuring that your journey is both enriching and responsible.

So, carry your spirit of adventure, your curiosity, and your enthusiasm for the natural environment. Be prepared to sample local food, immerse yourself in the Falklands' history, and capture magnificent scenes via your lens. Your Falkland Islands trip awaits, offering experiences that will last a lifetime and a strong connection to this distant and enchanting corner of the globe. Whether you're pulled by the call of nature, the attraction of culture, or the excitement of discovery, the Falkland

Islands have something exceptional in store for you.

Printed in Great Britain
by Amazon